THE ART OF BECOMING

When God Is the Artist

JOEL ESPINOZA

wichmann & co

Publishing House

Cover design: Isabella Santiago

Publisher: Wichmann & Co LLC, United States.
www.wichmannandco.com
hello@wichmannandco.com

ISBN (paperback): 979-8-9934623-7-0
ISBN (e-book): 979-8-9934623-8-7

First edition, May 2026, Printed in the United States of America.

CONTENTS

The Brushstroke Of Beginnings   2

1. Becoming Isn't Always Beautiful   7

2. Make Space   17
   God Can't Fill What's Already Full

3. When The Road Breaks, God Builds   27

4. The Secret I Hated, The Grace I Found   37

5. What Can You Make Out Of This, God?   47

6. Superhero Cape Not Required   57

7. Stormwalker   69

8. The Comeback Belongs To God   79

9. In Between Places   91
   When Hurt Met Hope And Healing

10. Now It's Your Turn To Tell Your Story   103

THE BRUSHSTROKES OF BEGINNINGS

S ome stories feel like unfinished sketches. Some beginnings are painful. Some paths feel like the world has gone silent, yet in the silence, the Artist speaks softly, calling you by name.

You might wonder, "Who is this Artist?" I'm glad you asked. His name is God.

This is one of those stories. Not because it's perfect, but because it's real. Because it's mine, and because it's yours, too.

I wrote this book for anyone who has ever felt unfinished, overlooked, or broken. For the one carrying shame, battling doubt, or questioning their purpose. For the one who feels like past mistakes have marked them permanently. For the one who wonders if God's plan will ever show itself in the middle of the mess.

I know those feelings well. I've wrestled with failure and shame. There were moments when the canvas of my life felt blank, like I had no idea what God was painting next. I've asked questions in the silence, wondering if anyone, even God, was listening. And yet, through it all, I discovered a truth that changed everything: When God is the Artist, nothing is wasted. Every broken moment, every misstep, every season of waiting is part of the canvas He is creating. Even the scars have meaning. Even the detours have purpose. Even the quiet can hold the promise of something new.

Think of Abraham, called to a place he had never been, asked to trust God even when the outcome seemed impossible. On the mountain, he lifted his eyes, and God provided a ram in the bush. God's plan didn't remove the journey or the struggle; He met Abraham in the process and shaped the story into a promise.

This book is a journey through valleys and victories. Through moments when I wanted to quit, when fear whispered louder than faith, when life felt unfinished and messy. It is a story of a God who shapes, restores, and transforms, turning brokenness into beauty and despair into purpose.

You'll read about times when I fell, about the lessons I learned in the quiet and in the chaos. You'll see how surrender, trust, and faith are not abstract ideas but lifelines that lead to restoration.

And I want you to know this: Your story is not over. No matter how dark the path feels. No matter how silent the world seems. God is still at work, shaping, forming, and creating in you.

This book is an invitation. To trust the Artist, even when you don't understand the process. To embrace the becoming, even when it's uncomfortable. To believe that every step, every struggle, and every scar is part of the masterpiece God is creating in your life.

And the Artist? He's still at work.

As God continued His work in me, He didn't just heal my heart, He restored something far greater. Part of that restoration was my family. My wife, Celia, has been one of the clearest expressions of grace I've ever experienced. The way she sees God, and the way she walks with Him, has shown me redemption and mercy in ways I never understood before.

He also entrusted me with three incredible kids: JJ, Joy, and Olivia. Each of them carries their own story, their own personality, and their own place in my heart. They're something special. Living reminders of God's goodness, mercy, and His commitment to keeping me humble and grounded... while still letting me believe I'm a pretty cool dad. You'll meet them later in these pages.

Your story isn't finished. It's just beginning.

CHAPTER ONE

Becoming Isn't Always Beautiful

As kids, most of us dreamed of having a perfect life. I remember telling everyone, "When I grow up, I'm going to be a doctor and have lots of money."

My parents worked hard for my brother and me. Their first home was in the Fair Park area of South Dallas. We didn't have much, but we always had food on the table. I remember my mom making us chicken sandwiches for our trip to Six Flags. We couldn't afford the food inside the park, but when it was time to eat, we ate well.

Back then, cartoons only came on during the weekends. One of my favorites was ThunderCats. I'd stand in front of the mirror, holding a toy sword and yelling, "Thunder! Thunder! Thunder!" derCats – HO!"

Watching my parents hustle day in and day out stuck with me. They taught me work ethic, sacrifice, and how to push through hard times. But as I got older, everything began to change. My interests, my priorities, and even my dreams. I wanted a future, but I didn't yet understand the cost of becoming someone who could handle it.

You might ask, "Why did your dreams change?" I think a lot of people can relate to my answer:

Dreams without direction eventually fall apart. Having big goals without guidance is like driving a car without insurance; one mistake, and everything can crash. Without someone helping you see clearly or steer in the right direction, things can fall apart fast. None of us know what life will look like ten or twenty years from now. So many of the choices we make don't turn out the way we expect.

Ever asked yourself: What if I was never supposed to date that person? What if I shouldn't have taken that job? What would my life be like if I had gone back to school and earned a degree?

I wasn't great at taking advice when I was younger. Like most teens, I thought I had it all figured out. Accepting advice felt like weakness, as if I were admitting I didn't know what I was doing. I remember someone once told me, "Don't date unless you have a job." I thought that was ridiculous. I figured love was enough. Spoiler alert: it wasn't. That mindset followed me into real life. I wanted grown-up blessings with a kid mindset. I wanted the package without putting in the work. I learned that lesson the hard way. I took a girl on a date to Olive Garden with only $20 to my name. Before you laugh or judge me, keep in mind, I had never been there before. I didn't realize how expensive it was, especially for a 16-year-old kid. When the bill came, reality hit. I was starving... but I just ate that salad while she enjoyed her pasta. It wasn't just about the money. It was the moment I realized I wanted things I wasn't ready for. I wanted a relationship without the responsibility, the dream without the discipline. Looking back, I wish I had listened. But more than that, I'm grateful I learned early, because becoming isn't just about what you want, it's about who you're willing to grow into.

One of the greatest lessons I've learned is the importance of staying open to the wisdom and experiences of others. I'm incredibly thankful for those who poured into my life. People who shared their stories, whether heartbreaking, challenging, or humorous. Those conversations shaped me. They molded my character and changed my perspective.

There's a saying I've come to live by: "If you want to grow in wisdom, listen to those who've walked a little further down the road." They've seen more. They've gone through more. And they carry wisdom that could save us pain, if we're willing to listen.

If there's one thing I know: Your scars don't disqualify you, they testify that God isn't finished with you yet.

Read that again. Don't let shame convince you your story has to stay hidden.

YOUR STORY MATTERS!

This book is about being real. About my journey, my failures, and my victories. My hope is that in sharing my story, you'll be reminded of how faithful God is, even when life doesn't make sense. Take a moment and reflect on your own life. Think about the choices you regret... the detours you've taken... the times you thought God was in it – only to realize later that you were running the show.

Can God still forgive that? Can He redeem it? Absolutely.

I think of the Israelites. Their journey from Egypt to the Promised Land was full of delays, bad decisions, complaints, and failure. But God never gave up on them. He was patient. He was merciful. And He still brought them to their destination. Just like them, your life may have detours, setbacks, and moments that don't make sense. Maybe you didn't expect your life to involve heartache or rejection. Maybe you've spent years asking, "Why me?" or "What did I do to deserve this?" But I want you to know: Your story isn't over. You might not have signed up for the struggle, but you were made to overcome it. And through it all, God is still writing something beautiful in your life.

Even if everything feels like it's falling apart; your home, your finances, your sense of identity, don't miss this: God is still writing your story.

As I started seeing my own story clearly, I began to see God's heart for others too. The same grace that never left me in my mess was quietly shaping my calling, long before I ever stepped behind a pulpit. I don't have all the answers. But I'm someone who's walked through pain and learned to lean on a faithful God. I'm here to remind you: Keep moving forward. Your promise is on the other side of the mountain.

My Yes Didn't Start with a Pulpit. Most people don't know this about me... I never imagined I'd one day preach or speak at different churches. I was just a young man with a heart to serve, even if I didn't have it all figured out.

At 18, I attended a Bible school in Mexico called Magdicl. I didn't know what my future held, I just knew I was hungry to grow, to learn, and to be used by God. My "yes" didn't start with crowds. It started on dirt roads, in small churches, in villages, even on buses. No microphone. No stage. No social media. Just a message of hope, and a God who was already moving. And to this day, I'm still amazed by the doors God has opened. I've spoken in rooms both big and small. Not because I'm the most gifted, but because He's faithful.

But let me be honest... I still have doubts. I've preached my heart out and walked away wondering, Did that even matter? I've seen empty altars. Quiet rooms. And I've asked God, Was I obedient? In a world of likes, shares, and platforms, it's easy to compare yourself to others. But God has reminded me again and again:

You weren't called to compete. You were called to be faithful.

Every time I speak, I do so by grace. I'm still learning. Still growing. Still depending on Him.

God Uses Imperfect People. Though my parents are from Mexico, English was my first language. I didn't learn Spanish until I lived there. And even now, when I preach in Spanish, I sometimes trip over my words. People say, "Your Spanish is great!" But inside, I know the struggle. Sometimes I stutter. Sometimes I feel out of place or insecure. But I've learned: God isn't looking for perfection. He's looking for obedience.

Here's something that's helped me keep going: What you're going through may not even be about you, it's about what God wants to do through you. That prayer you've been waiting on? That closed door? That struggle? It might be the very thing God uses to reach someone else. That doesn't mean He's forgotten you, it just means your victory is still in the oven.

I think about that when I watch my wife bake. She mixes every ingredient carefully, places the pan in the oven, and waits. But before the cake comes out, she takes a butter knife and pokes the center, to make sure it's ready. God does the same with us. He checks our hearts. He waits until we're ready from the inside out. Because the last thing He wants is to give us something too soon and watch it fall apart.

But some of my insecurity didn't start on a stage or behind a microphone. It started much earlier, long before I had words for it.

The Hardest Part of My Story. There's something I haven't shared yet. It's not easy to talk about, but it's important.

When I was a child, I was sexually abused by a man in our neighborhood. He offered me candy if I walked with him to the store. My mom was cooking. My dad was at work. I was riding my bike in front of our house. And just like that... my innocence was stolen.

I grew up guarded, angry, and full of fear. Trauma has a way of shaping how you see people. But that doesn't mean we have to live bitterly. It doesn't mean we're disqualified. As I got older, I realized I had a choice: I could let the pain destroy me... Or I could let God use it. It wasn't easy. Healing isn't instant. But by God's grace, I chose healing. And today, by His mighty hand, I'm standing here to tell you: God can use your scars too.

I don't share this part for pity. I share it because someone reading this might not know how to talk about their pain. And if my story helps them take one step toward healing, it's worth it. If you've walked through trauma, know this: Your story is not finished. Your pain has purpose. Your voice matters. Your testimony can bring healing. God isn't done with you.

All of this, the hurt, the fear, the mess you've carried, is not wasted. It's part of your story, and God is ready to take it, redeem it, and use it for His glory. Right now, you can surrender it all to Him.

Say this prayer and let it be a way of giving it to God and stepping into His plan for your life.

A Prayer of Surrender and Becoming

Becoming isn't always beautiful, but it is always purposeful when God is the one shaping you.

God,
Help me to see others through Your eyes.
Teach me to love like You love.
Help me forgive, even when it's hard.
Give me peace and patience in the waiting.
I surrender every part of my life to You, especially the parts I hide.
Heal what's still broken in me, even the things I don't talk about.
Remind me that my story isn't over, and that You can bring purpose out of pain.
Use my scars as reminders of Your faithfulness.
Give me courage to speak, even when my voice shakes.
Let my life point people to You, not to my strength, but to Yours.
Use my story for Your glory.
Amen.

CHAPTER TWO

Make Space
God Can't Fill What's Already Full

W hen It Rains, It Pours. Have you ever felt like life just keeps hitting you from every angle?

You've probably heard the phrase, "When it rains, it pours." If you're anything like me, you've had moments when everything feels heavy; your mind, your heart, your spirit. You've quietly said to yourself, alone in your car, "What else can go wrong?" or "God, what now?"

It's wild how quickly our minds can turn against us, filling with fear, anxiety, and worst-case scenarios. Even when people try to encourage you, all you can see is the pain, the pressure, the problems right in front of you. Life can feel crushing, like you're being hit from every side. But even in the storm, God is at work. He's there, inviting you to pause, lean into Him, and let His Spirit guide your thoughts instead of letting the chaos control you.

BREAKING THE CYCLE

So how do you break that cycle? How do you silence the noise and shift your thinking?

It starts by confronting what you've been feeding your mind. According to the Laboratory of Neuro Imaging at USC, the average person has 48.6 thoughts per minute – over 70,000 a day. That's a flood of information, emotion, and distraction. But here's the deeper question:

What are you allowing to live in your mind rent-free?

The Bible says:

> *"So prepare your minds for action and exercise self-control."*
>
> 1 Peter 1:13 (NLT)

Your mind needs direction the moment your feet hit the floor. Because if you don't command your thoughts, your thoughts will command you.

If you're driving to work in the morning and your spouse says something that hits a nerve, or a trigger shows up – pause. Don't snap. Don't say the first thing that comes to mind. Take a breath. Step back if you need to. And pray. Let God help you respond, not react.

You might feel like you've tried everything, but your emotions keep taking over. That's exactly why I start each morning with this simple prayer: "God, give me Your thoughts so I can think like You, and Your words so I can speak like You."

It's not a magic formula, it's a moment-by-moment surrender, trusting God to lead my mind and my words.

Scripture tells us:

> *"Take captive every thought and make it obedient to Christ."*
>
> 2 Corinthians 10:5 (NIV)

You may not be able to stop a thought from showing up, but you absolutely have the authority to decide what stays. Not every thought deserves access.

Your mind is like an inbox. Some messages are truth. Others are straight-up junk. And just like emails, toxic thoughts must be deleted. Your spirit can't thrive when your mind is overcrowded. You won't hear God clearly when your mental inbox is full of lies, shame, fear, lust, and bitterness. You won't see purpose when your vision is clouded by pain and people's opinions. Until you remove out what's killing your peace, you won't make room for what God wants to pour in.

Paul put it this way:

> *"Fix your thoughts on what is true, honorable, right, pure, and lovely."*
>
> Philippians 4:8 (NLT)

When your thoughts wander into darkness, flip the channel. Turn off "Channel Negative." Mute "Channel Fear." Tune into "Channel Hope." Choose to focus on truth, not trauma. Clearing your mind is the first step. True direction comes when you let God lead your steps and shape your purpose.

Lost Without Direction

Being lost isn't just about not knowing where to go. It's about making room. Room in your mind, your heart, and your spirit. Until you clear out the clutter, the lies, and the old labels, there's no room for God to pour in what He has for you.

Have you ever been on a road trip, completely lost, but too stubborn to stop and ask for directions? You keep driving, hoping something familiar pops up. That's how a lot of people are living right now. No GPS. No map. No direction. Just movement. But movement without purpose is just noise. You're running in place, not advancing. So let me ask you, how long have you been spiritually lost? How many months, or years have you been stuck in survival mode? Before you hit play on life again, ask yourself: "Do I really want to change?"

It's easy to point fingers. But real growth starts with an honest mirror. What's in me that needs to shift?

BREAKING FREE FROM LABELS

God has planted identity in you with roots deeper than every label spoken over your life. But the noise of the world; words, labels, and past wounds, can make it hard to recognize what He's placed in you.

I remember being in third grade, pulled out of class for speech therapy because I stuttered. Kids laughed. They called us "the slow group." And for a long time, I believed it. Because of my stuttering, I also struggled with a lisp. On top of that, I dealt with bad acne. Kids would say things like, "Hey, let's play tic-tac-toe with your face," or "Who ordered pepperoni pizza?" Those words cut deep and built layers of insecurity all around me.

What about you? What words have been spoken over you that you've made permanent? Who labeled you? Who lied to you?

Here's the truth: God's perspective outweighs man's opinion. Your healing begins the moment you start believing what He says about you. Knowing God's truth is only powerful if you choose to live it, if you choose to let it shape your life today.

But here's the catch... faith without action stays stuck. You have to want it. You have to want God's truth to shape how you think, how you act, and how you see yourself.

START NOW

If you're not happy with where you are, don't just complain about it. Do something about it. Not tomorrow. Not next year. Now. You don't need a New Year's resolution. You need a right-now revelation.

We've used our struggles as a reason to stay stuck for too long. We've made our trauma our personality. We've let the wrong voices drown out God's voice.

But I dare you to change the narrative. I dare you to speak life in the middle of your valley. Seeing yourself the way God sees you is just the beginning. Open your heart fully and let Him guide your steps. Don't just hear this, let God's truth take root in your heart. Let it shape your thoughts, guide your actions, and strengthen your steps through every season of your life.

A WAKE-UP CALL

This chapter isn't a motivational pep talk. This is a spiritual wake-up call. It's time to rise. It's time to let go of the clutter. It's time to take back your mind and reclaim your identity in God.

I've told myself some negative things over the years: "You'll never finish anything." "You're too inconsistent." "You're double-minded."

Even now, writing this, I'm breaking free from those chains.

And I want to tell someone reading this: the pity party is over. No more dark rooms. No more isolation. No more mental self-sabotage. God didn't give you a defeated mind. He gave you the mind of Christ.

> *"Let God transform you into a new person by changing the way you think."*
>
> Romans 12:2 (NLT)

You've probably said it yourself: "I need to change." You've looked for answers, asked for advice, and still felt stuck. The truth is, real transformation starts when you surrender to God. When you stop trying to fix it all on your own and let Him take the lead.

GO TO THE SOURCE

Remember this: You're not broken beyond repair. You're handcrafted by the Creator of the universe. The point is: if your car breaks down, you don't take it to a company that didn't make it. You go to the one who designed it.

So why are you reaching for temporary fixes... alcohol, sex, gossip, distraction, when the One who made you is patiently waiting? Stop trying to repair what only the Master Builder can rebuild from the foundation up. Go back to the Manufacturer. Let Him reset your mind, heal your heart, and restore your soul.

All the clutter, lies, and fear you've been carrying, they don't define you. You can release them to God. Let Him strip away the weight, restore your heart and mind, and fill you with His truth and His presence.

A PRAYER OF REMOVAL AND RENEWAL

God,
I've been asking, "What's next?"
But now I see You've already been preparing what's next all along.
Forgive me for letting my thoughts lead me into fear, doubt, and confusion.
I surrender my mind to You.
Clear out the clutter. Break down every lie.
Fill me with Your peace, Your truth, and Your voice.
Help me stop chasing counterfeit comfort, and run to the only Source who satisfies.
Create in me a new heart, ready for You.
I give You full access.
In Jesus' name,
Amen.

CHAPTER THREE

When The Road Breaks, God Builds

Have you ever driven down a road under construction, only to realize too late that you missed your exit? You're forced to take a detour, and suddenly, nothing looks familiar. Signs are missing. Lanes are closed. Your GPS keeps rerouting but can't seem to figure it out either.

I can't tell you how many times I've been in the car with my wife, and we both think we know exactly where we're going. I'll say, "It's the next exit." She'll say, "No, you already missed it." Before we know it, we're off course, in the middle of nowhere, just looking at each other like – oops.

That's exactly how life can feel sometimes. You think you're headed the right way. You've got your goals, your plans, and your timeline. But somewhere along the way, things start falling apart. Suddenly, nothing makes sense. The route you were on now feels like a confusing maze with no clear direction.

Many of us are in a season of construction where life feels torn up; marriage, ministry, finances, even your emotions. Just because your path looks messy doesn't mean you're lost. As the song reminds us, "I was lost, but now I'm found."

God never loses track of your journey. Even when your GPS is confused, God's navigation is still working.

I remember when Downtown Dallas underwent massive freeway reconstruction. New roads were added and old ones were rerouted, it was a mess. Life can look exactly like that. You're following the vision God gave you. You're reading His Word. You're staying focused. And then, loss hits, illness strikes, or doors close. Suddenly, you're asking, "Did I miss something?"

But the Lord says:

> *"See, I am doing a new thing! Now it springs up;*
> *do you not perceive it? I am making a way in the*
> *wilderness and streams in the wasteland."*
>
> Isaiah 43:19 (NIV)

Even when it feels like the road is breaking beneath you, God is building something greater. He opens doors in impossible places. He softens hardened hearts. He brings dead dreams back to life. Where you thought it was over, God begins again. He's not confused; He's constructing. And just like any construction zone, there's dust, delay, and discomfort, but the new road is always worth it. Don't Let Pride Make You Miss It. Sometimes we miss divine exits, not because God didn't speak, but because pride told us we didn't need to listen. We tell ourselves, "I know what I'm doing," or "I've got this."

Let me challenge you: think about the times you said, "I've got this." How did that turn out? Chances are, not the way you planned. That's because some things aren't meant for you to fix on your own.

If you're not an electrician, you don't rewire your house. If you're not a doctor, you don't self-diagnose. And if you're not God, you can't control everything. True wisdom comes when you stop trying to do it all yourself and surrender to the One who sees the full picture.

One day, I tried painting a small room by myself. It took me nearly three hours just to paint one wall. When my wife got home, I looked her straight in the eyes and said, "Let's hire a painter." We both laughed and knew – I had stepped outside my lane. That moment taught me something: Humility isn't weakness. It's wisdom.

> *"When pride comes, then comes disgrace, but with humility comes wisdom."*
>
> Proverbs 11:2 (NIV)

Some of us are stuck, not because God didn't open the door, but because our pride kept us from walking through it. Don't just swallow your pride. Surrender it to God. Saying "I was wrong" doesn't make you weak; it makes you free. Saying "I'm sorry" isn't a step backward, it's where healing begins.

When you stop guarding every wound, you invite God to step into the places that need healing most. Pain Can Blur the Path.

Sometimes, it's the hurt you've never healed that makes you miss life's exits, the ones you didn't see coming.

Hurt clouds everything. Your self-worth, your trust, even how you see God. It's like driving through a storm with no headlights. The road disappears. Your hands grip the wheel. All you want is to get through.

I believe pain has a voice. It tells you to hide. To stay silent. To pretend you're fine, so you don't get hurt again. But here's the truth: God doesn't run from brokenness. He moves toward it. He meets you where it hurts. Not with shame, but with healing.

> *"The Lord is close to the brokenhearted and saves those who are crushed in spirit."*
>
> Psalm 34:18 (NIV)

Your pain isn't a disqualification. It's preparation. It's a call to surrender. You can't be rebuilt if you keep holding on. Maybe it's trauma, bitterness, disappointment. You've carried it long enough. Today, give it to Him. Let Him restore what's been broken. Let Him heal what's been holding you hostage. Even King David prayed:

"Search me, God, and know my heart; test me and know my anxious thoughts. See if there is any offensive way in me, and lead me in the way everlasting."

Psalm 139:23 (NIV)

That's a bold prayer. It's like telling the Great Physician, "Scan every part of me. Show me what's wrong so You can make it right." Fear Can Paralyze You. When pain stays buried, it doesn't disappear, it turns into fear. Fear of being hurt again. Fear of losing control. Fear of what might happen next.

Have you ever been so anxious that you couldn't even breathe? I've been there. I've had panic attacks behind the wheel, feeling like something terrible was about to happen for no reason. I've sat at work, silent and overwhelmed, just hoping no one could see how much I was struggling.
Anxiety can become a silent driver. It'll steer your life if you let it. But that's the moment, right in the middle of that panic, when you can turn it over to God. Not after you've fixed it, not once it all makes sense, but right there, hand in hand with Him, letting His peace meet your fear.

"Do not be anxious about anything, but in every situation, by prayer and petition, with thanksgiving, present your requests to God. And the peace of God, which transcends all understanding, will

> *guard your hearts and your minds in Christ Je-*
> *sus."*
>
> Philippians 4:6–7 (NIV)

I've felt that peace. The kind that makes no sense in your situation but calms your spirit like nothing else can. When I talk to God, I feel like a child climbing into their Father's lap, safe, secure, and seen. Let God Be Your Guide.

Let me be real: there are no shortcuts to healing. But there is always a way forward. If you've missed the exit... if you feel broken, ashamed, or lost... God hasn't given up on you. He's still building. He's still rerouting your life. Not to delay you, but to develop you. Let Him guide you back to purpose. When He says, "Take this exit," trust Him, even if you can't see the full road ahead. He's not just restoring you; He's making you new.

You are approaching your destination. Keep going. You have arrived.

A Prayer for Roadside Redemption

God,

I admit there have been times I thought I knew the way. Times when pride told me I didn't need help. Times when pain blinded me and fear paralyzed me. But today, I surrender. I give You my detours. I give You the exits I missed, the opportunities I wasted, and the shame I've carried. I give You every broken piece of my story and ask You to rebuild me from the inside out.

Search my heart. Expose every anxious thought, every hidden wound, and every false identity I've held onto. Tear down what needs to be torn down. Heal what's been hurting. Clear the clutter, the confusion, and the noise until I can hear Your voice again.

Lead me back to purpose. Even when the road looks unfamiliar, help me trust that You are still in control. Remind me that what feels like a delay is often Your preparation. Give me the boldness to exit where You lead, even if I can't see what's on the other side.

Thank You for never leaving me stranded. I believe You're not just fixing my path, You're building something brand new.

In Jesus' name,

Amen.

CHAPTER FOUR

The Secret I Hated, The Grace I Found

A few years ago, my wife gave me a brand-new iPad. I loved that thing! It got used so much it eventually wore out. Fast forward to a recent Christmas: we visited family in Arizona, and on the day we arrived, she surprised me with a new iPad. I was hyped. Like a kid on Christmas morning hyped.
Over the next few days, I hunted for the perfect case. I didn't want a scratch or crack. I even tried using the old one, but it didn't fit. You can probably guess where this is going.

One afternoon, my mother-in-law said she had a surprise for me. While she talked, the iPad rested on my lap. I opened her gift. a nice sweater and jeans. I jumped to hug her, and in slow motion, I watched the iPad slide off my lap and slam face-first onto the floor.

Everyone froze. I stood there, heart sinking. When I finally picked it up, it was exactly what I feared, the screen was shattered. As I stared at the broken iPad, it hit me: this small device was a mirror of my life with God, showing how easily I dwell on what's broken instead of focusing on Him.

THE SHAME OF BREAKING WHAT WAS GIVEN

I felt awful. Not just because it broke, but because my wife had just given it to me. I felt like I let her down.

How many times do we do the same with God? We mess up what He's given us; a promise, a relationship, or a chance to do what's right, and shame hits hard. We get stuck looking at what's broken instead of leaning on His mercy and running back to the One who gave it.

> *"Each of you has been blessed with one of God's many wonderful gifts to be used in the service of others. So use your gift well."*
>
> 1 Peter 4:10 (CEV)

Everything we have; our talents, our time, our story, comes from Him. Nothing is random, and nothing is just for us. Every ability, every word, every act of love is meant to overflow into the lives of others. Your voice, your creativity, your ability to listen, encourage, build, teach, serve, or simply show up with love. You don't just carry a gift. You are a gift, intentionally placed in this world to make a difference that only you can make.

WHAT'S YOUR GIFT?

Maybe you're gifted in leading, encouraging, teaching, cooking, fixing things, or serving. Whatever it is, it wasn't given just for you. As mentioned in 1 Peter 4:10: God has given each of you a gift from His great variety of spiritual gifts. Use them well to serve one another. Don't hoard it. Don't waste it. Don't bury it.

God gives us gifts, but shame, fear, or hidden struggles can hold us back from using them. I know because I've been there.

Some of us have locked away our gifts because of pain. Hurtful experiences at church, disappointment, or drifting from God. But His heart towards you hasn't changed. He gave you that gift for a reason. Stop believing the lie that your time is over, that you're washed up, or that you're stuck in your past. His mercy is fresh every morning, and He's ready to help you use what He's entrusted to you.

MY SECRET STRUGGLE

This isn't just about a broken iPad or talents. It's deeper. It's personal. It would be easy to say I've always gotten it right, that I've always walked free. But that wouldn't be true. I know what it's like to carry a gift in one hand and guilt in the other. To serve publicly while struggling privately. Maybe that's you too? Smiling on the outside while hiding something you don't know how to release.

I've loved sharing God's Word since I was a teenager. I've preached in cities I never imagined visiting, crossed paths with people who've changed my life, and served in ministry for over 25 years.

On the outside, it looked like everything was going right. But the truth is, ministry success doesn't erase the battles we fight in secret. There was a season when I was carrying a hidden burden, something I was ashamed to admit: pornography. Yes. While in Bible college. While serving in ministry.

It began as a quiet curiosity. A moment I thought I could control, but that silently pulled me into a storm. I was 19, at a friend's house, when I saw something I knew I shouldn't. My hands trembled, my chest pounded, and every part of me screamed to stop... but I pressed play anyway. In that instant, a door swung open, and I had no idea how tightly the chains behind it would grip me. That one choice became a hidden stronghold, holding me captive for years, invisible to everyone around me.

Pornography became my secret escape, my hidden habit. A kind of poison I turned to whenever I was stressed, discouraged, or feeling spiritually dry. I even got married thinking it would just go away, but it didn't. The trap stayed tight. I smiled in public, I preached, I served. But behind closed doors, I was hurting, weighed down by shame and guilt. If you've ever carried a secret like this, especially in ministry, you know what it's like to feel completely alone.

What I struggled with in the shadows didn't just stay in the shadows. It spilled into my marriage, my ministry, and who I thought I was at the core. Hidden sin and secret shame are like silent earthquakes; they shake everything, even the parts of your life that seem solid. They eat away at trust, joy, and peace, quietly messing with everything you care about.

The Cost of a Secret Life

Maybe your struggle isn't pornography. Maybe it's alcohol, drugs, gossip, anger, or shame. Maybe you've convinced yourself God's done with you, that He can't forgive you, can't use you, that your mistakes have written the final chapter of your story.

That's a lie straight from hell. Satan's goal is to steal, kill, and destroy, but Jesus came to give us life; real, full, overflowing life that nothing and no one can take away (John 10:10 NIV).

Here's the truth: you're not disqualified. You're not too far gone. Your calling is not canceled. You've just been listening to the wrong voice, the one whispering doubt, fear, and shame. Secret struggles make you feel completely alone, like no one could ever understand what you're going through. But God sees you. He knows every hidden corner of your life. His mercy is bigger than every mistake, every slip, every secret you've tried to bury. You don't have to keep hiding. You don't have to pretend. You don't have to let shame write the story of your life. You can step into the light, surrender it to Him, and let God restore what's been broken.

LET GOD RESTORE WHAT'S BEEN BROKEN

I know the feeling of being bound… feeling like a puppet to sin, trapped in a cycle you can't escape. But I've also experienced what happens when you surrender it all to God.
You stop running. You stop hiding. You stop faking. And you let God rebuild you from the inside out.

For me, restoration didn't happen overnight. God brought people into my life who could speak truth, hold me accountable, and walk with me through the process. I learned to pray consistently, stay in tune with Him, read the Word, and surrender this struggle every single day. I also learned not to entertain the enemy. If I need to flip the channel, scroll past, or just look the other way, I do it. It's a daily choice, but each time I do, I feel freedom and healing seep in a little deeper.

Just like the broken iPad, the value of the gift doesn't change because it's cracked. It's still yours. But now it's time to honor it, protect it, and take it back to the One who gave it to you. Say: "God, I broke it. But I want it restored."
He's not mad. He's ready. And when you let Him restore what's been broken, you realize His love, mercy, and grace are stronger than every failure, every shame, every chain.

So today, take that step. Hand Him what's broken in your life. Surrender the shame, the secret struggle, the guilt you've been carrying. Find someone you trust, like your pastor, a mentor, or a close friend, who can walk with you through this journey. Let God restore you. Let Him rebuild you, piece by piece, and step into the freedom and purpose He has for you. Don't wait another day, start now.

A Prayer from the Secret Place

God,
I've carried shame and silence for far too long.
I've buried gifts You placed in me, gifts meant to bless others.
I've run from You when I should've run to You, hiding in fear, guilt, and regret.
Today, I surrender it all.
Heal what's broken in me.
Revive what's been buried under shame, regret, or fear.
Remind me that even with cracks and flaws, You see value in me.
Give me the courage to step into the gifts You've entrusted to me.
Help me protect them, nurture them, and use them to glorify You.
Help me walk in freedom, live with integrity, and never let shame speak louder than Your grace.
Surround me with people who can encourage, speak truth, and hold me accountable.
Keep me close to Your Word, steady in prayer, and sensitive to Your Spirit.
When temptation comes, remind me to turn away, flip the chan-

nel, and fix my eyes on You.

Restore me, God. Rebuild me, piece by piece. Let Your love, mercy, and power flow through the cracks and make something beautiful.

In Jesus' name,

Amen.

CHAPTER FIVE

What Can You Make Out Of This God?

Have you ever looked at your life and thought, "What could God possibly do with someone like me?" Not just something you think once and move on from, but a real question that sits with you. One shaped by your story, your mistakes, and everything that feels unfinished.

That question isn't new, and it's one I've brought to God more times than I can count, and He's never turned away.

There's a story in the Bible, found in Jeremiah 18, that has always stuck with me. It compares God to a potter and us to clay. Clay doesn't start out impressive, it's messy, shapeless, and ordinary. But in the hands of a skilled potter, it can be formed into something meaningful and useful. The shaping, the spinning, the pressure, even the moments that feel like crushing, aren't wasted. They're all part of the process, turning a simple lump of clay into a work of art filled with purpose. And that's where many of us get stuck.

The truth is, most of us count ourselves out before God ever gets a word in. We replay our past, zoom in on our failures, and get stuck staring at the mess right in front of us. We start telling ourselves things like, "God can't use someone like me," "I don't have anything left to give," or "My time is up – I'm too old now." But that's not how God sees you.

Scripture says:

> *"But the jar he was shaping from the clay was marred in his hands; so the potter formed it into another jar, shaping it as seemed best to* him."
>
> Jeremiah 18:4 (NIV)

That's grace in motion. The clay didn't turn out the way the potter expected, but he didn't throw it away. He didn't walk away. He reshaped it. He started again. God isn't waiting for you to get it all right; He's waiting for you to let go.

That's what I've had to learn too. Handing over my doubts, insecurities, and weaknesses to God, again and again. I've told Him more times than I can number, "Here I am. Use me." And what still surprises me is this: it's usually in my most tired, broken, and insecure moments that I see Him move the most. I've stepped up to preach feeling unsure, thinking, "What if I mess up? What if the words don't come out right? What if I start stuttering?" And yet God shows up every time, filling the room in ways I could never explain.

That's the Potter at work.

And He's still working in me. Shaping my thoughts, my emotions, my heart, my mind, my body, my soul. He hasn't finished. And neither has He with you.

THERE'S MORE IN YOU THAN YOU REALIZE

So many of us walk around carrying untapped potential, weighed down by words spoken over us years ago – "You'll never amount to anything." Others keep repeating the lies to themselves: "I'm not qualified. Not smart enough. Not talented enough."

I get it. I've said the same things in my own mind and even in prayer: "Joel, your Spanish is not the best. Your English is broken. Just stay quiet. You stutter when you're nervous, you need help." That fear, that voice of doubt, can feel so loud. But those lies didn't come from God, they came straight from the enemy, because he knows exactly where to hit you.

And that's exactly what Moses felt when God called him. He tried to talk God out of using him, listing every reason why he wasn't the right guy. Yet God already knew his weaknesses, and still called him.

Just like Moses, God looks beyond our doubts, flaws, and fears. He sees both the person we are now and the person we can become, and He calls us anyway. He's not waiting for us to have all the boxes checked off; He's waiting for us to show up and let Him work.

Could it be that He's calling you into ministry? Could it be that He's asking you to serve your community, your workplace, or your own family? Could it be that He wants to take your story, the very part you've been ashamed of, and use it to bring hope and encouragement to someone else?

Whatever it is, He can, and will, use you, exactly where you are. The Potter is still at work, shaping, molding, and refining you. Every twist, every press, every gentle spin, it's all part of His plan to bring out the purpose He's placed inside you. You may not see it yet, but He's not finished, and He never wastes a single moment of your story.

HE GOES WITH YOU

Here's the part we often forget: God doesn't just call you, He goes with you.

This verse always gets me:

> *"The LORD replied, 'I will personally go with you, Moses, and I will give you rest – everything will be fine for you.'"*
>
> Exodus 33:14 (NLT)

God didn't send Moses immediate support. He didn't hand the journey off to someone else. He said, "I'll go with you." Into your work. Into your purpose. Into the unknown. Into the moments that feel uncertain.

And He doesn't just promise presence, He promises rest. Strength for the road. Peace for the pressure. Think about the last time you felt overwhelmed, unsure, or stretched beyond what you thought you could handle. You weren't alone – and God hasn't left you now.

Don't stress about having all the answers or trying to figure it out on your own. Don't Google it, don't overthink it. Just trust that the Potter is still at work, and the One who calls you is walking right alongside you. God didn't tell Moses, "Sorry, this is hard, I'll make it easy for you." No. He said, "I'm with you. I'll give you what you need. Everything will be fine." Not because you have it all together, but because He does.

WHEN THE TASK FEELS TOO HEAVY

I remember working on a major project in the past. It was overwhelming. Long nights, constant pressure, moments when I honestly felt in over my head. But I kept showing up, because I knew walking away wasn't an option, and I trusted God would carry it all.

When the project was finally finished, it turned out to be a huge success. In a meeting afterward, someone asked me, "How did you pull it off?"

My answer was simple: "God gave me the wisdom. I owe it all to Him."

At the time, I didn't understand why I had to face so much pressure. But looking back, I see the bigger picture. It wasn't really about the project at all. It was about trust. It was about learning, once again, that God is faithful. He really does finish what He starts. Every late night, every stressful moment, every challenge, He used it to shape me, to teach me reliance on Him, and to show me that even when the task feels too heavy, He's carrying everything. Let God Use Your Whole Story.

"Your imperfections are actually a good thing. People don't grow from strengths; they grow from weaknesses... When you admit your imperfections – when you're real with others – people draw closer to you."

Rick Warren

Think about that for a second. You don't have to hide your scars. You don't need to pretend. God isn't asking for a polished version of you, He's asking for the real one. Your weakness doesn't disqualify you. It makes you relatable. And God gets the glory through your growth.

So stop hiding. Let God mold you. Let Him shape you. Let Him remake you.

If you haven't stepped into a church in a while, I know what you might be thinking, or even joking about: "If I go back, the whole building's gonna collapse." I get it. You feel too far gone.

Unworthy of redemption. Like your past is too embarrassing to talk about and your story feels too complicated for anyone to really understand.

The truth is, the roof won't cave in when you walk through the door, but heaven just might. Because when a heart comes home; like the prodigal returning after years of wandering, lost and broken, ashamed of the mess made along the way, something shifts. God runs to meet you, arms wide open. Celebration erupts in heaven. Grace floods in. The one who thought they were too far gone is welcomed back, not with judgment, but with love and forgiveness.

Picture the Potter at His wheel, hands on the clay, spinning, pressing, shaping. With every touch, He's forming something deliberate, something intentional. He shapes not just the whole, but every detail, including your name, your gestures, your body, your eyes, your hair, the way you move. I can imagine Him looking at His work and saying, "There's no mistake in this. This is exactly what I planned. I'm pleased with what I'm creating." Every flaw, every crack, every part of your story is in His hands, and He's smiling over the masterpiece He's shaping: you.

A Prayer in the Potter's Hand

God,

If You can do something with me – here I am.

I won't explain why I'm not ready.

I won't negotiate my way out of the call.

I surrender. I'm clay in Your hands.

Keep shaping me, even when it hurts.

Keep walking with me, even when I can't see the full picture.

Thank You for not giving up on me.

Thank You for choosing me, flaws and all.

Help me step into the story You're writing with my life.

Help me embrace my weaknesses, share my scars, and let You use my story to heal others.

Surround me with people who speak truth, hold me accountable, and encourage me to keep growing.

Amen.

CHAPTER SIX

Superhero Cape Not Required

Have you ever felt like time was already ahead of you, like the day started and you were already behind before your feet even hit the floor?

That's been one of the biggest areas God has had to work on in me: my time. Not just how I spend it, but how much pressure I pile on myself.

Some mornings, I wake up and my mind is already racing: mow the lawn, get an oil change, hit the barbershop, help around the house. Every little thing feels urgent, like it all has to happen before breakfast. And just like that, before the day even starts, I feel stretched thin.

Night finally comes. My body's tired, but my brain won't quit. The to-do list keeps replaying, the pressure builds, and patience is long gone. Sound familiar?

That's when it hits me... it's not just busyness. It's overload. Doing more, producing less, carrying more than I should.

If you're trying to get the family ready for church on Sunday, you get it. Or on a Monday, trying to wake the kids, get them dressed, and out the door for school, especially when they're moving in slow motion.

Life can feel heavy no matter your stage; work demands, family responsibilities, helping friends, checking in on parents, managing your own health, or just keeping up with everyday chores and bills. There are seasons when it seems like everyone and everything wants a piece of you at the same time. It's exhausting. Sometimes, it feels like you're drowning.

And then there's that moment you think you're "Superman", expected to have it all together. You glance in the mirror, flex your invisible cape, and realize... you're exhausted. No matter what role you're playing, that cape doesn't make you invincible.

You're Not Alone in the Pressure

Some mornings, just getting out of bed feels like a battle. That superhero cape, meant to make you unstoppable, suddenly feels heavy. Some days, you wake up tired, worn out, and realize it can't make you superhuman.

Maybe you just left the doctor's office with a life-changing diagnosis. Or maybe you're at the grocery store, silently putting items back because your card won't cover it all.

When life feels like it's dragging you under, it's easy to think you're the only one struggling. But the truth? Everyone deals with pressure like this sometimes.

So if that's you right now, I want to pause and say it clearly:

You're not alone. Everyone, yes, everyone, has moments when life feels like too much. And the good news? God is right there with you in the middle of it. He hasn't stepped away. He's holding you, even when it doesn't feel like it.

I know what it's like to worry, to feel afraid, to wonder how you're even going to make it through. I've been there too. Let me show you what that looked like in my life.

A SEASON OF LOSS

I remember a season when I was working for a company with crazy hours. I'd clock in at 6 a.m. and leave close to 8 p.m. The grind was brutal, and after a while, it started wearing me down. Then one day, right before lunch, my boss called me into the office. I thought, Here comes that raise I've been working for. Nope. I got let go. Yeah, you heard that right. After everything I poured into that job, they said they didn't need me anymore.

I walked out thinking about my wife, my kids, the bills, and the shame. The walk to my truck felt forever. I didn't even know how I was going to tell my wife. But the moment I called her, before I could speak, she said: "You got let go, didn't you?" I was like, Wait... how did you know? Then she said something I'll never forget: "It's okay. Come home."
Those words brought a peace I can't describe. Life hits hard sometimes, but that doesn't mean you're alone. God often shows up in the quiet, simple moments. Even when it feels like

the world is crashing down, everything really is going to be okay.

Come home.

IT'S NOT THE END. IT'S THE BEGINNING

Maybe a door just closed for you. Maybe you're asking, What did I do to deserve this?
Please hear me! This isn't the end. This might actually be the start of a brand-new chapter.

When I got let go, I was bitter. I thought, I worked so hard. I gave so much... and this is how it ends?

But God? He's faithful. Eventually, He opened a better door. A job closer to home, a role where I got promoted, even leading a bilingual team across the nation. He gave me better. But I had to walk through the valley first.

Sometimes the struggle isn't punishment, it's preparation. Every long night, every challenge, every moment of uncertainty, every question running through your mind. He is shaping you, equipping you, teaching you to rely on Him.

I'm reminded of a boxer in the middle of a fight. Round after round, he's getting hit, stumbling, thinking it's over. He's about to give up. Then, out of nowhere, something clicks. He digs deep, finds strength he didn't know he had, and swings with everything left in him. Suddenly, the fight turns. What felt like the end just moments ago becomes the start of a comeback.

Life's like that too. You feel beaten down, ready to throw in the towel. But God is still at work behind the scenes, giving you timing, strength, and courage. What looks like the end might actually be the moment everything starts to change.

So keep sowing, even when you don't see results. Keep moving forward. Keep trusting Him. You might not see it yet, but God is quietly working, turning your story into something far greater than you imagined.

KEEP GOING

> *"Plant your seed in the morning and keep busy all afternoon, for you don't know if profit will come from one activity or another – or maybe both."*
>
> Ecclesiastes 11:6 (NLT)

Life can feel like a stack of little efforts; emails, errands, prayers, conversations, acts of kindness. You might not see results right away. You could be one moment away from a breakthrough.

*"There are better things to do than succeed, more
important things to do than make it in the world,
and there are worse things to do than fail…"*

Pastor David Gibson

Keep trusting. Keep stepping forward, even when you can't see the full picture. And then God moves. Quietly, powerfully, in ways you didn't expect. That's when you feel it: His presence, His faithfulness, His hand guiding every step. It's not just accomplishments, it's His Spirit whispering, I've been with you the whole time.

YOUR EMOTIONS CAN DECEIVE YOU

Let's be real. Too often, we start with how we feel instead of starting with God. It's time to declutter your emotions.

Think of your mind like a crowded closet. Stress, fear, doubt, and past mistakes all piled in, weighing you down. Decluttering means handing it over to God. Give Him the worry, the fear, the replayed mistakes.

When you do, you make room—for peace, clarity, and His guidance. Say it out loud: "God, I give this to You. I don't need to carry it anymore." Little by little, the weight lifts. Not because the problems disappear, but because He's carrying them for you.

When was the last time you truly stopped, just sat still, and remembered how faithful God has been?

• The time He provided groceries when your account was empty.

• The accident you should never have walked away from but survived.

• The door you never saw coming but He opened anyway.

Now, invite Him into the quiet of your heart and mind: "God, I give You this fear. I give You this anxiety. I give You this burden."

Notice... I didn't say my fear or my anxiety. When we claim it as ours, we carry it alone. But God never meant for you to carry it by yourself. Hand it over.

• Instead of saying, "my depression," say, "God, I give this to You."

• Instead of, "life feels hopeless," say, "God, life feels heavy, but I trust You with it."

When you do, something shifts. The burden hasn't disappeared, but the One who holds all things is now holding it for you. Your shoulders aren't carrying it anymore, He is. Peace steps in. Faith grows. The Spirit of God says: You are not alone.

"O God, my heart is quiet and confident."

Psalm 57:7 (TLB)

When your heart is fixed on Him, fear, anxiety, and doubt lose their grip.

SPEAK TRUTH OVER THE NOISE

The enemy loves to plant lies, especially before your feet even hit the floor. Thoughts about people, problems, deadlines, or the future can start spinning before your day even begins.

Here's what I've learned: don't let your thoughts run the show. Meet them with God's truth.

"Do not be anxious about anything..."

Philippians 4:6 (NIV)

God isn't just telling us to "calm down." He's inviting us to stop letting worry control us. Bring it to Him; stress, doubts, and "what-ifs." When we do, His peace fills the space anxiety used to occupy.

So I pray right there in bed, saying: "Lord, my thoughts are all over the place. But You've got this. Bring me peace."

A Prayer to Let God Be the Hero

God,

Some days feel like everything is falling apart. I give my all, but it still doesn't feel enough. I try to hold it together. For family, work, everyone, but inside, I'm tired, overwhelmed. Honestly... sometimes I just want to quit.

But You see me. You hear the prayers I don't even speak. You catch the tears no one else notices. You know the weight I'm carrying, and You never expect me to carry it alone.

Today, I hand over what I cannot control. The fear, the worry, the pressure to be strong. Calm my racing mind. Steady my heart when it feels like it's breaking. Remind me I don't have to be perfect, just present. Help me breathe. Help me trust that You're in this with me. Help me believe You're still writing my story, even on the hard days.

I surrender the rush. I surrender the pressure. I surrender the lie that I have to do it all on my own. Lead me... and I will follow. One step at a time.

In Jesus' name,

Amen.

CHAPTER SEVEN

Stormwalker

Peter asked for the humanly impossible, and that's bold faith. He and the disciples had been fighting wind and waves all night when Jesus appeared, walking across the water. The storm was raging, and the water was rough. Yet Peter did exactly what Jesus said. He stood up, stepped out of the familiar, and walked straight toward Him... on water.

Let's be clear: Peter didn't just step into the water, he walked on it. By faith, he did what no one else on that boat even dared to do. An ordinary man doing something extraordinary. That moment had nothing to do with skill or experience, it was about a heart willing to trust and obey Jesus.

Your life might feel shaken, thrown off balance, or rocked by the storm right now, but you'll never see what God can do until you step beyond what feels comfortable. A comfort zone isn't always wrong, it's just familiar. Predictable. Safe. And sometimes it quietly holds you back from the growth God wants for you. Maybe it's a job that drains you but feels secure. Maybe it's fear of failure that keeps you from trying again. Maybe it's a routine you cling to because change feels risky.

God is calling you into something bigger, something that

stretches your faith. Staying where you are may feel safe, but it keeps you from seeing the miracle God wants to work. The storm isn't there to crush you; it's there to teach you how to rely fully on Him. When you step out, even when fear is loud, that's when you experience what Scripture calls pistis. The Bible often translates it as faith, but it's more than just believing something is true. Pistis is active trust. It's confidence that moves your feet. Faith that steps forward before everything makes sense. It's faith that puts weight on what Jesus said and lives like He meant it. Peter didn't stand on the water because he believed in himself. He stood because he trusted the One who called him. That's pistis. Not passive belief, but obedience in motion.

And right there, when things feel uncertain and unstable, when the waves feel like they're dragging you down, that's where Jesus meets you. Not after the storm stops. Not once you feel brave enough. He meets you in the middle of it and keeps you from going under. (even when it feels like the waves are dragging you down).

WHAT'S YOUR BOAT?

The boat represents whatever you cling to for security. It's the thing you fall back on because it feels safe. Maybe it's your own self-reliance – thinking you've got it all under control, rather than trusting Him. Maybe it's the life you know instead of the calling God has been stirring in you. You hesitate because fear speaks up: What if it fails? What if people judge me?

But Jesus is saying, Step out. I've got you.

The storm doesn't make you sink. It's what you focus on that takes you down (when your eyes shift from Jesus to the chaos around you, fear starts to feel heavier than it is). Peter didn't start sinking because the water couldn't support him. He began to go under the moment he stopped looking at Jesus (his faith shook, and suddenly the waves seemed to pull him down).

"But when he saw the wind, he was afraid and, beginning to sink, cried out, 'Lord, save me!'"
Matthew 14:30 (NIV)

Notice, it wasn't the water. It was the wind: invisible, yet intimidating. That's exactly how fear works. It starts unseen and quietly drags you under (slowly, almost without warning, until you realize you're overwhelmed). Peter was a fisherman. He had weathered storms before and could tell the difference between rough water and real danger. Yet this time, relying on his instincts almost cost him a supernatural moment.

I've been there... depending on my own strength instead of God's promises. When I did, I felt myself going under (emotionally, spiritually, mentally). But just like Peter, when I cried out, God reached for me.

Take this to heart: calling out is just the first step. The next step is staying the course. Faith, pistis, grows when you keep your eyes on Him in the storm and trust Him even when everything feels shaky, unstable, or impossible. That's where heaven touches earth, and God's power shows up in ways you never imagined.

So let me ask you today: What's your boat? What are you holding onto because it feels safe, even if it's keeping you from what God has for you?

KEEP YOUR EYES ON JESUS

"Let us keep looking to Jesus. Our faith comes from Him and He is the One who makes it perfect."
Hebrews 12:2 (NLV)

Picture Peter again, standing on water with chaos all around him. The moment his focus shifted, fear moved in. That's exactly what this verse is pointing to. The word keep isn't casual. It means persistent focus. Don't glance. Don't check in occasionally. Lock your eyes and heart on Jesus, especially when things feel unstable. Your faith, your next step, your peace depend on it.

And notice this: faith comes from Him. Peter didn't create courage on his own. He trusted Jesus, and it was enough. Faith doesn't require perfection; it starts in Him.

"Perfect" doesn't mean flawless. It means complete. Fully equipped. God takes whatever faith you bring. Small, shaky, even fragile, and strengthens it. When Jesus said, "It is finished," He showed us that everything needed for faith has already been provided. All that's left is to look, trust, and move forward. So in the middle of your storm, the instruction is simple: keep your eyes on Jesus. Don't stare at the waves. Don't let fear steal your focus. Just keep looking at Him.

TRY AGAIN

Maybe you've stepped out before. You started strong, but the pressure increased. Fear crept in. You wondered if staying safe would be easier.

Try again.

This time, don't just step out. Stay focused. Let Jesus be your fixed point when everything else feels unstable. Don't let distractions steal what God is doing. Don't let other voices drown out His. Don't let anxiety or insecurity pull you back.

Faith, pistis, isn't the absence of fear. It's choosing to keep going, knowing the One who called you hasn't left you. Every shaky step stretches your faith. Even the smallest act of trust meets the strength of God. Fear doesn't disqualify you. It often becomes the place where God demonstrates His power.

So what are you waiting for? Start again, even if it didn't work last time.

FAITH VS. DOUBT

When Peter started to sink, Jesus didn't turn away. He didn't shame him. He reached out immediately. "You of little faith, why did you doubt?"

The Greek word for doubt, distazō, means to be divided. It's like trying to walk in two directions at once. Faith moves forward; doubt pulls you apart. But doubt doesn't disqualify you.
In Mark 9:24, a father cries out, "I do believe, help me overcome my unbelief!" That prayer is raw, honest, and real. And Jesus responds with healing. God honors surrendered faith, even when it's mixed with fear. Doubt isn't the opposite of faith; it's often the doorway to deeper dependence. It's the honest prayer, "Lord, I believe, help me. I can't carry this on my own."

Your Turn to Walk

What are you holding onto? What has you locked in fear? Is God calling you forward, but safety feels easier? Jesus didn't rush Peter. He didn't shout. He simply invited him, step by step, at the pace of trust. This is your moment.

Step out. Keep your eyes on Jesus. Trust Him when the wind is loud. And just walk. Your step doesn't have to feel solid or secure, just pointed toward Him.

A Prayer to Step Out of the Boat

Jesus,
I've stayed in this boat long enough.
You're calling me out, and honestly, I'm scared.
The wind roars. The waves crash. My faith feels small.
Yet I hear You say, "Come."
So here I am, stepping out. Not because I'm ready, but because I trust You.
Help me focus on You when fear tries to shout louder than faith.
Help me walk when the path is unclear.
Forgive me for the times I let doubt silence Your voice.
For the moments I looked at the storm instead of the Word.
Thank You for never letting me sink.
Thank You that when I called, "Save me," You reached out.
In my weakness, You are strong.
When I'm falling apart, You hold me together.

I surrender fear, pride, and excuses.

I will no longer try to walk in two directions.

Today, I choose to walk toward You; by faith, not by sight.

When doubt comes, pull me close.

I'd rather be drenched in a storm with You than safe and dry without You.

In Jesus' name,

Amen.

CHAPTER EIGHT

The Comeback Belongs To God
Running On Empty

Some people have been fighting for so long, they're just done. Checked out from life. Maybe that's you. Not just physically, but deep in your soul. Life feels stuck on pause, and somewhere along the way, you stopped dreaming. Stopped hoping. Stopped expecting anything good. So you started settling. Settling for whatever job pays the bills. Settling for relationships that offer a little attention, even if they're unhealthy. Settling for the idea that failure is just part of your story now. You know that feeling, like your car is struggling, running on empty, and every mile takes everything you've got. That's what life feels like when disappointment, fear, and exhaustion have been piling up for years. You keep moving, but barely. You're surviving, not really living.

And that's when the questions start creeping in: Is this really my life? Was I actually born to live this way? Is this all there is?

Follow me in this chapter, because I believe God wants to answer those questions... and remind you that this isn't the end of your story.

THE WEIGHT OF THE PAST

Earlier in this book, I shared how I grew up with a speech impediment. It messed with more than just my words, it messed with how I saw myself. I remember kids laughing when I had to leave class for speech therapy. It wasn't just embarrassing. It made me feel like something was wrong with me. And I didn't know how to stand up for myself. Every time I got nervous, I'd start stuttering. And that stutter made me feel… Small. Insecure. Like I didn't belong. Like I didn't have a voice.

Now I'm 46. And even though I've done a lot of healing, there are still days when I look in the mirror and see that 10-year-old boy again. It shows up before a big presentation at work. Or when I'm about to preach somewhere new. Or when I walk into a room full of people I don't know, and that old fear sneaks in. And here's what that voice says: "You're still that stuttering kid. Nothing's changed. No one wants to hear you."

That voice hits hard, doesn't it? Telling you to quit, hide, stay safe, stay small. You feel it in your chest, your shoulders, your heart.

But here's the truth. You weren't meant to fight this with your own strength. God sees it all, and He's ready to step in. Trust isn't enough. Real freedom comes when you release it all. Every fear, every doubt, every worry, into His hands every single day. God didn't design you to go at it alone. This was never meant to be Joel versus the world.

LET GOD FIGHT

So how do you keep going when your mind is all over the place and your heart feels completely worn out? How do you even take the next step when the past keeps whispering in your ear, reminding you of every failure, every wrong turn, every "what if"? Here's the question God put in front of me one day: Are you trying to fight this battle yourself... or are you gonna let Me handle it?

In the Bible, there's an incredible story: a whole nation, thousands of men, women, and children, had just been set free from years of slavery. They were exhausted, worn down, and finally tasting freedom. But now... they were completely cornered. Pharaoh's army was closing in. There was nowhere to run. And in front of them? A massive, seemingly impossible sea. Waves stretched as far as the eye could see. Panic was rising. Fear pressed in from every side. The people started to complain. Nearly 500,000 adults and children, all overwhelmed and scared, questioning how they would survive.

And in the middle of that chaos, God said something that flipped the script:

"The Lord will fight for you. All you have to do is keep still."

Exodus 14:14 NLV

No battle plan. No weapons. No clue what would happen next. Just: stand still and trust Me. That's exactly what God does. He might call you to step up and act. Other times... He says, "I've got this. Stay still."

THE POWER OF STILLNESS

Being still can take more courage than swinging, shouting, or running. It's not about proving your point. It's about trusting God when everything in you wants to fight. Stillness doesn't mean doing nothing. It means choosing to let God lead when everything in you wants control. It's staying quiet when someone pushes your buttons. It's loving the person who hurt you. It's choosing prayer when panic feels easier.

That last line of Exodus 14:14 gets me every time: *"All you have to do is keep still."* The word "keep still" in the Bible isn't about freezing or doing nothing. It's about pausing in trust—choosing to stop trying to control everything and letting God take the lead. It's a posture of surrender, not passivity.

I know... being still is hard. When everything around you is loud. When life feels like it's spinning out of control. When your emotions are all over the place. But stillness isn't weakness. It's trust. It's believing before the breakthrough even shows up. The Israelites had to believe the sea would move. They had to trust that stepping out wouldn't be the end. Stillness is a kind of faith that moves before anything moves. Fighting without fighting or fighting back doesn't always look like force, anger, or losing control. Sometimes it looks like not giving in. Not giving in means you keep showing up when nothing seems to change. You still pray, even when the words come out broken. You still worship, even when your heart feels heavy and tired. You still choose obedience, even when it costs you comfort, convenience, or control. That's the kind of fight David understood. Not just swinging a sword, but learning how to trust God in the unseen moments, when strength had to come from somewhere deeper than himself.

That's why he could say:

> *"He is my strength, my shield from every danger.*
> *I trusted in him, and he helped me.*
> *Joy rises in my heart until I burst out in songs of*
> *praise to him."*
>
> Psalm 28:7 TLB

Because when the fight is quiet, God becomes your strength. That's why his worship was bold. Because his victories didn't come from skill. They came from his Savior.

Worship and faith aren't just for the Psalms, they are weapons that should be active in every battle of your life. God Shows Up. Trusting God sounds good... until life gets real. Until you're running low on funds. Until the fridge is almost empty. Until your kid is running far from God and you don't know how to reach them. Until your marriage feels cold, distant, and quiet. Faith isn't tested when it's easy, it's tested when need is right in your face and answers feel far away.

I remember a season when I got sick and couldn't work for months. No backup plan. No extra savings. Just bills, fear of what's coming next, and long nights. Money was tight. As a parent, you try to stay strong for the kids while quietly wondering how you're going to make it. I prayed a simple, desperate prayer: "God, please show up." Not fancy. Not theological. Just honest.

The very next day, a couple we didn't even know knocked on our door, holding bags of groceries. Not random items. The exact cereal our kids liked. The exact things we needed. They said, "God gave us your name and address. He told us to bless you." I couldn't hold it together. I stood there and cried. Because in that moment, it wasn't about food. It was about being seen. It was about God reminding us, I know where you live. I see what you're facing. I haven't forgotten you. God saw us. God showed up. And the truth is, He was already moving before we even knew what to ask for.

That's how God works. He doesn't always show up early. He rarely shows up on our timeline. But He is always right on time. When you feel stretched thin. When you're running on empty. When you're wondering if your prayers are even reaching heaven.

Remember this: God is already working behind the scenes, lining up provision, help, and grace you haven't seen yet. You might feel alone. But you are not unseen. And you are never forgotten.

STOP TRYING TO FIX EVERYTHING

Some of us are just wired to try to fix everything. It's in our nature. When life goes sideways, our first instinct is to control, to plan, to micromanage every little thing. We try to patch the problems, smooth the chaos, and make it all work, because giving up control feels like failing. Sometimes the hardest, but most freeing thing you can do is stop trying to fix everything and just let God be God.

Life has a way of piling on, doesn't it? Bills, deadlines, expectations, fears... and we start thinking we have to solve it all ourselves. But here's the truth: we weren't made to carry it all on our own.

If you lost your job; fight back by applying again, yes, but also trust God's not finished with your story. If your kid's off course; fight back with prayer and love, not guilt. Let God do what only He can do. If people are talking; fight back by staying quiet, walking in integrity, and letting God defend you.

Because at the end of the day: God doesn't need your help. He wants your faith. Your effort matters, but it's not your comeback He's waiting on. You don't have to make it happen.

So if you feel like you're at the end of your rope, holding on with everything you've got, don't tap out. Your comeback isn't on you. Your breakthrough isn't in your hands. Your victory isn't about proving you can do it alone. Your comeback belongs to God. And here's the beautiful part: when you let go, He doesn't just step in. He shows up in ways you couldn't imagine. Doors open you didn't see. Words fall into place. People appear in your life exactly when you need them. He moves when you can't. Let Him fight. Let Him lead. And watch Him turn what felt like the end into your greatest beginning.

A Prayer: God, Take the Fight

God,

I'm tired of pretending I'm strong when I feel like I'm falling apart. I've been swinging at shadows, fighting battles that aren't mine and it's left me empty. I've carried shame, fear, and voices that keep calling me by my past.

But You're calling me by my purpose. So today, I surrender. I lay down the pressure. I lay down the need to prove myself. I lay down the lie that says I have to figure it all out. I don't want to fight in my own strength anymore. I want to move when You say move and be still when You say be still.

Remind me I'm not alone. Remind me You're already in the middle of this. Speak louder than fear, insecurity, and defeat.

I give You the fight. I give You the fear. I give You the comeback.

This isn't just another chapter in my story. This is where You step in. The comeback belongs to You.

In Jesus' name,

Amen.

CHAPTER NINE

In Between Places
When Hurt Met Hope and Healing

S ome folks try to live in the present, but the past still holds them captive. It's like a tug-of-war. You step forward, but something keeps yanking you back, reminding you of every mistake, every loss, every "if only" moment.

Here's the truth: problems never leave you the same way they found you.
When you look back, you realize you're not the same person anymore. Maybe there are more wrinkles or a few gray hairs, but that's just surface-deep. What's deeper is how life's experiences have shaped you. Some parts of you have hardened; others have softened. You've been stretched in ways you didn't know you could handle.

Maybe you used to smile freely, but bitterness has moved in. Maybe you were the life of the party, but now people hesitate to invite you anywhere because all you talk about is pain. Maybe joy feels like a visitor, coming and going before you can even catch your breath. You're stuck in between places, not fully in the past, not fully in the present.

Can you relate?

THE SAMARITAN WOMAN

There's someone in the Bible who was in that exact place.

> *"Soon a Samaritan woman came to draw water, and Jesus said to her, 'Please give me a drink.' He was alone at the time because His disciples had gone into the village to buy some food. The woman was surprised, for Jews refuse to have anything to do with Samaritans. She said to Jesus, 'You are a Jew, and I am a Samaritan woman. Why are You asking me for a drink?'"*
>
> John 4:7–10 (NLT)

Because of her culture, her background, and her gender, she was shocked that Jesus, a Jewish man, was talking to her.

Here's what we know about her:

• She was alone.
• She had been married five times and was now living with a man who wasn't her husband.
• Her reputation in town was bad.

She wasn't just drawing water, she was carrying years of shame, rejection, and failed relationships. She was surviving day by day, quietly, avoiding the world's eyes and side comments. Her story may look different from yours, but the weight feels the same. You may not have had five ex-husbands, but many of us know what it's like to avoid people, dodge places, and feel labeled for life. We've carried shame in secret, pretending everything is okay, quietly wondering if anyone could ever really see us, or love us for who we are.

The Samaritan woman's courage was quiet. She showed up at the well, alone, in the hottest part of the day, carrying all her burdens. Sometimes, just showing up, even for a moment, is the first step toward freedom.

A Chapter I Never Planned

Like the Samaritan woman, I can relate... to some extent. There was a season in my life when I faced one of the hardest challenges I've ever known: divorce. I know what it feels like to be completely isolated, trapped in shame, guilt, and loneliness. You walk through the world carrying invisible weight, afraid of judgment, afraid of being misunderstood, afraid even to look in the mirror. I wrestled with whether to share this part of my life. Some told me to skip it, Divorce is a topic people shy away from – too painful, too messy, too 'unspeakable.' People might see you differently. But I feel led to include it here, knowing some of you may be walking that same road.

I understand the sting of judgment and the heaviness of feeling like a failure. But if you've encountered divorce, or any heartbreak, know this: God is present even in the hardest moments. Surround yourself with supportive people; pastors, counselors, friends, family, mentors, because healing doesn't happen in isolation.

Let me be clear: I am not for divorce. Marriage matters deeply to God. It was His idea before it was ever ours. I believe in fighting for covenant, praying through hard seasons, seeking wise counsel, and inviting God into places where love feels thin and hope fragile. Marriage is holy work, and sometimes the greatest act of faith is staying and believing God can heal what looks broken.

But I also believe in telling the truth.

Sometimes, despite every prayer, every tear, every attempt at reconciliation, things still fall apart. Not because God failed. Not because grace ran out. But because we live in a fallen world with broken people, layered wounds, and real consequences.

If you're reading this carrying the weight of what didn't work, hear this: your story is not disqualified. It is not over. It is not beyond God's ability to heal, redeem, and use for His glory.

FINDING HOPE AND HEALING

Believing that truth doesn't happen overnight. For me, it came after everything fell apart. When the noise settled, and I was left face-to-face with my own heart. I had a choice: stay stuck in regret or let God begin the work of restoration.

I had to find myself again. I intentionally leaned into God through prayer, fasting, reading Scripture, and rebuilding relationships that had been strained or neglected. Some days felt strong and hopeful; other days felt quiet and weak, but I kept showing up. I made the decision daily. To draw closer to Him and focus on healing, not shame; restoration, not regret. I stopped replaying what went wrong and asked God what He wanted to rebuild.

And here's what I learned: when God restores you, He doesn't just patch up what was broken. He reshapes how you love, how you trust, and how you show up. Healing doesn't erase your past, it redeems it. Restoration asks for honesty and humility, letting God work in places only He can reach.

That work mattered, because I didn't want to repeat old patterns in a new season.

God's Restoration in Our Family

Over time, God brought restoration and new beginnings. I remarried an incredible woman, Celia, we call her Cel. Together, we've built a marriage rooted in faith, trust, and intentional love. Lord willing, this year we'll celebrate 12 years of marriage May 30.

It wasn't quick. It wasn't comfortable. It required honesty, humility, and daily effort. We took a 12-month Christian marriage course and committed to living out what we learned every day. The work transformed our marriage and strengthened our family.

Our blended family is a true blessing:

• JJ moved back home and is currently attending church with Celia, Olivia, and me. I'm proud to see him serving God through youth ministry, worship, and even helping with general work around the church. It's amazing to witness the man he's becoming and know that God has incredible plans for his life. He's planning to propose soon to his love, Isabella, who also played an important role in this book by designing the book cover and also took the photos.

• Joy also attends church where she currently lives. She loves to be challenged, is fiercely intelligent, and never ceases to amaze me. I love my girl and continue to believe that God will fulfill His purpose in her life in amazing ways.

• Olivia, or Oli as we call her at home, is funny, curious, and full of energy. She's just starting high school, has joined the youth worship team, and is our family baker, always ready to whip up something sweet.

Our family isn't perfect, but it's a living picture of God's restoration, His grace, and the beauty of second chances.

THE WELL MOMENT

Most Jews avoided Samaria, even though it was the shortest route to Galilee. Tension ran deep. But Jesus didn't avoid it. He went straight to meet one woman.

> *"If you only knew the gift God has for you and who you are speaking to, you would ask Me, and I would give you living water."*
>
> John 4:10 (NLT)

Friend, God has a gift for you, living water:

- Living dreams
- Living joy
- Living peace
- Living purpose
- Most importantly, salvation

Sometimes we're so focused on our pain that we miss Him standing right in front of us. We come to Jesus with our needs, our hopes, and even our brokenness, not realizing that He's ready to meet us in the middle of our struggles. Before change can happen, He has to confront the truth of our hearts.

THE CONFRONTATION

"Please, sir, give me this water! Then I'll never be thirsty again, and I won't have to come here to get water."

John 4:15 (NLT)

She was ready for change, but Jesus confronted her truth: "Go and get your husband." She replied, "I don't have a husband." Jesus answered: "You're right! You don't have a husband, for you have had five husbands, and you aren't even married to the man you are living with now. You certainly spoke the truth!"

The truth can hurt. But it's the only way healing begins.

Aren't you tired of temporary fixes? Feeling better for a moment, only to fall back into the same place?

Jesus met her at the well, not to shame her, but to confront her truth enough to set her free.

RESTORATION

*"The woman left her water jar beside the well and
ran back to the village, telling everyone, 'Come and
see a man who told me everything I ever did!'"*

John 4:28 (NLT)

She left her past. She left her pain. She left her shame. Then she ran to tell everyone about the One who changed her life. That's restoration. When you can talk about past failures without shame, because they now bring glory to God.

God wants to take you from that fruitless in-between place into a life flowing with living water. He's inviting you to step forward, to let go of the past, and to receive the fullness He's offering. This isn't just about wishing for change, it's about opening your heart and saying yes to His work in your life.

Are you ready?

A PRAYER FOR HEALING AND NEW BEGINNINGS

God,

I come to You with an open heart. You know the places I've been stuck; in pain, in my past, in the shadows of my struggles. Lord, breathe into those broken places. Heal my wounds, restore my heart, and refresh my soul.

Jesus, You met the Samaritan woman at the well when she was lonely and carrying shame. Meet me here in my brokenness. Help me release every burden, regret, and piece of guilt at Your feet. Break every chain and fill me with Your living water, hope, peace, purpose, and joy. Show me Your presence in the middle of my struggles, and give me courage to take steps forward, even when it's hard or scary.

Father, I give You my past, my pain, and my story. I receive Your healing and new life. Transform my heart so I can love well, forgive freely, and live fully. Turn my scars and struggles into a story of Your grace that brings life to others.

I will walk in freedom. I will embrace joy. I will shine Your light wherever I go. I declare that Your plans are higher than mine, and nothing that is broken is beyond Your power to restore and make beautiful.
In Jesus' name,
Amen.

CHAPTER TEN

Now It's Your Turn To Tell Your Story

You've heard my story. The battles, the valleys and the victories God has given me. I've shared both struggles and wins; not to glorify myself, but to show how God moves in real life and to ignite what He wants to do in you.

Now, it's your turn.

Your story is far more than events or feelings. Every scar, tear, and moment you thought you'd never rise carries divine purpose. God is not just writing a story, He is building His Kingdom through your life. Even when you can't see it, He is at work, and your life can be a strategic tool in His hands.

Remember: if Jesus came to redeem a broken woman in Samaria, He can come into your home, your heart, your life today.

You may feel marked by your past, trapped by shame, or weighed down by failure. But the living God is greater than every chain. Your story is far from over. It is a battlefield, and God is inviting you to walk in victory.

THE POWER OF YOUR TESTIMONY

Your story carries God's power. It is a weapon that can break chains, awaken faith, and shift lives. This is not about self-help or motivation, it's about the authority of God moving through your obedience.

When you step out of the shadows and declare what God has

done in your life, He moves. Your testimony becomes a piercing arrow in His hands, able to confront darkness and bring breakthrough to someone silently struggling. Someone out there is waiting for hope, and your story could be the turning point they need.

> *"They triumphed over him by the blood of the Lamb and by the word of their testimony."*
>   Revelation 12:11 (NLT)

Every hardship, tear, and "how could this happen?" moment is not wasted. It is fuel. It is proof that God triumphs over every battle. Speaking your story is just the beginning. Letting God guide your words is where true impact begins. Your testimony is His tool, speak it boldly, and watch Him move. Sharing your journey opens the door; stepping into courage allows your life to become a heavenly weapon that impacts a generation.

EMBRACE YOUR VOICE

I know it's not easy. Your past might sting. Your wounds may still feel fresh. Sharing your story can be terrifying. What if people judge me? What if they don't understand?

But God does not call the qualified; He calls the willing. Even the messy, broken parts of your life can declare His glory. Your story can awaken faith, ignite courage, and dismantle the lies of the enemy.

When you speak honestly, you partner with God to move in ways beyond your imagination. Every testimony is a sword against fear, shame, and hopelessness. It reclaims what the enemy tried to destroy and declares that your comeback in the Lord will surpass your past setbacks. Do not underestimate what God can do through your honesty. Your brokenness becomes a stage for His glory, and His power shines brightest in weakness. Embracing the courage to speak transforms your life from a private struggle into a Kingdom tool, a declaration of God's power, freedom, and victory. Follow God's guidance, and watch your story turn from a chain into a sword, a force of deliverance for you and for others.

YOUR STORY IS A WEAPON, NOT A BURDEN

You're not defined by your mistakes or failures, you're defined by God's love. Every scar, every regret, every "I wish I'd done that differently" moment is not wasted. God can take all of it. The messy, painful moments that feel like they broke you and turn it into something powerful that can help you and others.

> *"Let the redeemed of the Lord tell their story – those he redeemed from the hand of the foe."*
>
> Psalm 107:2 (NLT)

Your story isn't a chain, it's a pathway. When God guides you, even the hardest moments can become tools for freedom. Every scar becomes a testimony. Every battle becomes a guide for someone else. Every triumph points to God's glory. Telling your story isn't optional, it's Kingdom work. Each truth you speak pushes back against lies, strengthens the weary, and lights the way for someone else to experience freedom. Your story is a sword, cutting through shame. It's a banner, waving hope in the darkness. It's living proof that God redeems what was broken. Let God transform hurt into healing, mistakes into wisdom, and scars into testimony. Every part of your journey can shine, showing His glory and bringing freedom to anyone who needs it.

When you step fully into the story God has written through

your life, you walk in freedom, a life no longer weighed down by fear, shame, or regret. Every scar becomes a story worth telling. Every struggle becomes a lesson someone else can use. Every victory becomes a beacon of God's glory. Your story has power. It has purpose. And when you share it, you are advancing the Kingdom, one real, honest word at a time.

THE ROAD AHEAD: LIVING IN GOD'S FREEDOM

The path ahead won't always be easy. Challenges will come, doubts will rise, and the enemy will try to whisper lies. But you do not walk alone. God goes before you, surrounding you with His presence and leading you into true freedom. Freedom from shame, fear, and every lie the enemy tries to plant in your mind. Jesus is knocking at the door of your heart. If you haven't surrendered your life to Him, now is the perfect moment. His blood redeems, His Spirit transforms, and His love breaks every chain.

"If you openly declare that Jesus is Lord and believe in your heart that God raised him from the dead, you will be saved. For it is with your heart that you believe and are made right with God, and it is with your mouth that you openly declare your faith and are saved."

Romans 10:9-10 (NLT)

Salvation is a transfer from death to life, a complete new beginning. I invite you to pray this prayer with me:

"Lord Jesus, I believe You are the Son of God. I believe You died for my sins and rose again. I surrender my life to You. Thank You for saving me and making me new. In Jesus' name, Amen."

If you prayed that, welcome to God's family! Your story has entered a new chapter. One filled with authority, freedom, and Kingdom impact.

Salvation is the doorway, but walking through it is where life truly begins. God hasn't just saved you, He's inviting you to live in the fullness of His freedom every day. Freedom isn't just a feeling; it's a choice, a lifestyle, and walking step by step with God's guidance.

Now that God is in your heart, it's time to take intentional steps to connect with Him, surround yourself with believers, share your story, and walk boldly in His purpose. The freedom you've received in Jesus is meant to overflow. Into your life, your family, and the lives of those around you. The action plan ahead isn't a checklist; it's a roadmap for living victoriously and fully free through God's presence and guidance. Here's how to get started:

YOUR ACTION PLAN

1. **Connect with God Daily.** Spend intentional time praying, reading Scripture, and listening for His voice. Even a few minutes each day can change your perspective, strengthen your faith, and guide your decisions. Start with the Gospel of John to see the life and teachings of Jesus up close. Journaling your thoughts or prayers can help you notice how God is speaking and working in your life.

2. **Join a Church Family**. Surround yourself with believers who will sharpen, support, and walk with you in faith. Look for a church that teaches God's Word in a way that's easy to understand, encourages growth, and actively lives out His truth. Get involved in a small group, Bible study, or ministry where you can build real relationships, ask questions, and serve others. Being part of a community helps you stay strong in your faith, offers encouragement during spiritual battles, and gives others the chance to be inspired by your journey.

3. **Declare Your Story.** Share your journey with someone you trust. Your testimony has power! It can awaken faith in others, challenge the enemy's lies, and bring freedom to someone who feels trapped. Don't wait for perfection; honesty and transparency are more pow-

erful than polish. Start small, then expand as you gain confidence.

4. **Live with Kingdom Purpose.** Ask God to guide your steps in everyday life. Make intentional choices that align with His Word, walk boldly in your calling, and be aware of opportunities to serve and bless others. Purposeful living turns ordinary moments into Kingdom impact.

5. **Stay Faithful in Battle.** Opposition and challenges will come, but stand firm. Philippians 4:13 (NIV) reminds us: "I can do all this through Him who gives me strength." When difficulties arise, pray, hold onto Scripture, and remember that each challenge is shaping your faith and preparing you for greater influence.

6. **Guard Your Mind and Heart.** Protect what you let in. Meditate on God's Word, replace negative thoughts with truth, and reject the enemy's lies. Your mind and heart are the foundation of your freedom. Fill them with truth, encouragement, and God's promises.

7. **Equip Others.** Look for ways to mentor, encourage, or share what you've learned. Your experiences, faith, and victories can help someone else rise. God often uses your story, wisdom, and guidance to impact lives in ways you may never see.

These steps aren't just tasks to check off, they're ways to live out the freedom and new life God has given you. Each action draws you closer to Him, strengthens your faith, and equips you to impact others. As you practice connecting with God, walking in community, declaring your story, and living with purpose, you're preparing for the next step: stepping fully into your story and letting it shine for His Kingdom.

CLOSING PRAYER

Father God,

Thank You for being faithful through every season. Today, I choose to step out of fear and shame and fully embrace the story You are writing in me.

Give me courage to declare Your truth boldly. Heal every wound, break every chain, and release me into the freedom You have for me. I declare I am redeemed, restored, and equipped by Your Spirit to impact lives.

Guide my steps daily. Surround me with Your presence and people who will walk with me. Replace doubt with certainty, fear with faith.

I will walk in Kingdom authority. I will live in freedom. I will declare Your power wherever I go. Nothing broken is beyond Your restoration.

Use my life as a weapon for Your glory.

In Jesus' name,

Amen

ABOUT THE AUTHOR

 Joel Espinoza is a speaker and author from Dallas, Texas. His life is a testimony of God's love to save, heal, and restore. After walking through seasons of brokenness and redemption, Joel carries a message that calls this generation back to identity, truth, and the transforming power of Jesus.

He shares the gospel with a Spirit-led authority that connects deeply with people and reminds them that their past does not disqualify them from the future God has prepared. Joel's passion is to see people break free from what once tried to define them and step fully into the life God created them to live.

Joel's greatest ministry is his family – his wife, Celia, and their three children, JJ, Joy, and Olivia, who remind him daily of God's faithfulness.

The Art of Becoming is Joel's debut book.

LET'S CONNECT

Joel Espinoza is available for speaking engagements, retreats, conferences, and ministry events.

EMAIL:

joelespinozaministries@gmail.com

FACEBOOK:

https://facebook.com/JoelEspinozaMinistries

INSTAGRAM:

https://instagram.com/JoelEspinozaMinistries

www.ingramcontent.com/pod-product-compliance
Lightning Source LLC
Chambersburg PA
CBHW071347150726
47997CB00002B/888